PATTON'S ONE-MINUTE MESSAGES

General George S. Patton Jr.

PATTON'S ONE-MINUTE MESSAGES

Tactical Leadership Skills for Business Management

Charles M. Province

★
PRESIDIO

Copyright © 1995 by Charles M. Province

Published by Presidio Press
505 B San Marin Dr., Suite 300
Novato, CA 94945

Library of Congress Cataloging-in-Publication Data

Province, Charles M.
    Patton's one-minute messages : tactical leadership skills for
business management / Charles M. Province.
        p.   cm.
    ISBN 0-89141-546-7 (pbk.)
        1. Patton, George S. (George Smith), 1885–1945—Quotations.
    2. Industrial management—Quotations, maxims, etc.   I. Title.
    E745.P3PP758   1995   95-11869
    658—dc20   CIP

Except where noted, all photographs are courtesy U.S. Army.
Typography by ProImage

Printed in the United States of America

This book is dedicated to my British friends: Dick Francis, the master of mystery writers; Lt. Col. (Ret.) George Forty, author and Patton authority; Captain (Ret.) George and Myra Killip, Great Britain personified; Kenn Oultram, British Patton Society founder; and George P. Kimmins, Patton Appreciation Society founder.

War is conflict. Fighting is an elemental exposition of the age-old effort to survive.

- It's the cold glitter of the attacker's eye, not the point of the questing bayonet, that breaks the line.
- It's the fierce determination of the driver to close with the enemy, not the mechanical perfection of tank, that conquers the trench.
- It's the cataclysmic ecstasy of conflict in the flier, not the perfection of his machine gun, which drops the enemy in flaming ruin.
- Yet, volumes are devoted to armaments; and only pages to inspiration.

It lurks invisible in that vitalizing spark, intangible, yet as evident as the lightning—The Warrior Soul. The fixed determination to acquire The Warrior Soul, and having acquired it to either conquer, or perish with honor, is the Secret Of Victory.

George S. Patton Jr.
The Secret Of Victory, 1926

Contents

Preface

George S. Patton Jr. was not superhuman. He wasn't born with stars on his shoulders. He was as mortal as anyone else in the world. He was just a guy doing his job—a job that he loved. He knew that to be a great commander he had to act like a great commander. He knew what it took to be the best in his field. He had no illusions, no prejudices. He was one of the great pragmatic leaders. He knew that a leader must not only act the part, he or she must become the part.

Although Patton was born neither a general nor a soldier, he determined at a very early age what he wanted to be. Once that decision was made, he never stopped working toward his goal. He trained himself, molding his personality and his philosophy, by immersing in the role of a great warrior, finally becoming what he wished to become. He worked at it and imbued himself with the warrior spirit. As he often said, "As a man thinketh so is he."

The purpose of this book is to indoctrinate readers with the Patton philosophy to such an extent that they will never stop aspiring to their goals; and to show that through perseverance, study, and eternal desire anyone can become great. As the general often said, "If a man thinks war long enough, it's bound to have a good effect on him."

Although this is a short book, it isn't meant to be read and done with in a day. Don't just read the book in one sitting and think you're finished. Read one maxim per day. Read it and *think* about it within the context of your personal experience. Think about what's being said. What does it mean to you? What does it mean in the context of your business or profession? What does it mean in the context of your life?

When you've given the book a great deal of thought and come to some personal conclusions, you may discover that you know people similar to the ones referred to in the text. You'll probably notice situations and conditions in your company that are in need of rectification. That's going to be the easy part.

The difficult part will be doing something about it. That's where Patton's one-minute-messages on perseverance and leadership come in. No one is going to do it for you. You're going to have to do it on your own, using your own initiative and drive.

In this text, exchange the following words:

supreme commander	=	CEO
headquarters	=	the boardroom
commander	=	manager
soldier	=	employee
victory	=	market share
maneuver	=	marketing
enemy	=	foreign manufacturers
killing	=	producing the best product

This book will not make you a great general or get you promoted to top level management in your company. No book can do that. Life is too unfair to make all capable, qualified people top managers. The book will, however, help you learn to discipline yourself. It will show you how to transform into a no-nonsense manager who can make good, sound decisions. It will help you become a person with good leadership skills who can recognize those skills in others. If opportunity knocks, and you have the necessary skills, you'll be ready to answer the door.

As you read this book, don't think only in military terms. Think also in business terms.

- Replace the concept of victory with the idea of putting a quality product on the market before your competitor.
- Replace the concept of war with the idea of making your quality product the standard for the market.
- Replace the concepts of casualties and death with the idea of layoffs and bankruptcy.

It's not hard to do, especially when you realize that business is synonymous with war.

I've started each page with a direct quote from General Patton. Each and every one delivers a distinct, powerful message concerning a quality of leadership and effective command that is sadly lacking in the American business community today. Following each of Patton's quoted maxims, I've written a one-minute message—a succinct clarification of the explicit meaning of that maxim using the Patton style and approach.

Although the messages following the quotes are my words alone, I've tried my best to write them as I think the general would have written them. After almost thirty years of studying Patton's philosophy and writing style, I feel comfortable doing so.

The Patton quotes come from a variety of sources:

Martin Blumenson. *The Patton Papers.* 2 vols. Boston: Houghton-Mifflin, 1972–74.

George S. Patton Jr. Gen. *War As I Knew It.* Boston: Houghton-Mifflin, 1947.

Porter B. Williamson. *Patton's Principles.* Tucson: MSC, 1979.

Fred Ayer Jr. *Before the Colors Fade.* Boston: Houghton-Mifflin, 1964.

Charles R. Codman. *Drive.* Boston: Little, Brown, 1957.

George S. Patton Jr. *The Secret of Victory.* Library of Congress, 1926.

Deming's fourteen points, seven deadly diseases, and obstacles are from:

W. Edwards Deming. *Out of the Crises.* Cambridge: MIT, 1982.

Mary Walton. *The Deming Management Method.* New York: Dodd, Mead, 1986.

I've written these one-minute messages using the military environment to keep their original flavor and context. Some of them need no translation from military to business concepts. These concepts are basically the same in both environments. Some of them, however, don't translate well upon first reading. When are translated idiomatic expressions from one language to another, true meanings are often lost. This also happens with translations of professional languages—e.g., when a doctor uses the word *discomfort* he really means pain. In these instances, some thought must be given to Patton's message and how it can be associated with the business community. In some cases, to make sure the translation is correct, I've added a second paragraph that will offer specific insight into the use of the message in the business community.

As I began to write this book, I felt as though I had already read these same words before or at least something similar to them. There was something vaguely familiar about some of the messages, something I hadn't considered while focusing specifically on my study of General Patton and his philosophy. I pulled W. Edwards Deming's book, *Out of the Crisis,* from my bookshelf and began to leaf through it, making comparisons between Patton's one-minute messages and Deming's fourteen points, seven deadly diseases, and obstacles. To my surprise, I discovered that many of the principles are the same. My initial surprise subsided when I realized that fundamental principles are universal. It doesn't matter whether they're conceived in the mind, observed from nature, or learned from experience. They do not change. Patton believed it is the job of the high command to provide the best quality it can in leadership, materials, supplies, and judgment. Deming reiterates that concept when he says the philosophy of producing quality must come from the top. It can't be done by the worker on the line, and it can't be accomplished by middle management. If there is no commitment from the top leadership of a company to produce the best quality product, using statistical quality control, there won't be any quality. Quality can't be inspected into a product after it's manufactured.

Patton knew, as does Deming, that good management is not enough. Along with management, the company must have good leadership, and if anyone knew about leadership, it was General George S. Patton Jr. He would have made one hell of a businessman.

Introduction

PATTON'S CAREER

Patton was many things to many people. Those who disliked taking orders thought him to be a thorough, out-and-out bastard. Those who understood the need for discipline and leadership thought him to be a great leader.

Following in the tradition of both his father and grandfather, Patton entered the Virginia Military Institute at the age of eighteen. He accepted an appointment to the United States Military Academy at West Point after one year at VMI because upon graduation he would automatically receive a commission in the United States Army.

In 1909, he graduated forty-sixth in a class of 103. He had held the ranks of cadet corporal, sergeant major, and adjutant. He won his school letter by breaking a school record in the hurdles event. Upon graduation, he became a cavalry officer and soon afterward married a charming young lady from Massachusetts named Beatrice Ayer. Her family was immensely wealthy. Beatrice's father, Frederick Ayer, owned the American Woolen Company.

In 1912, Patton attended the Olympics held at Stockholm, Sweden, the same year a young American Indian named Jim

Thorpe made history by winning and dominating the games. Patton competed in the modern military pentathlon. The events included pistol shooting, a three-hundred-meter swim, fencing, a steeplechase, and a cross-country footrace. He finished a very respectable 5th place.

After the games, and at his own expense, Patton traveled to the French Cavalry School located at Saumur, France, to take lessons from the fencing instructor there. He purposely cultivated his own reputation as a swordsman, and he later designed the M-1913 saber, which was adopted by the U.S. Army cavalry. Long before he became known as Old Blood and Guts (a name he hated), he was known as Saber George. For a very young second lieutenant, it was a great distinction.

Upon assignment to the Cavalry School at Fort Riley, Kansas, Patton took over instruction of the cavalry course, where he taught the use of the new saber he had designed. His title was master of the sword. He was the first to hold this newly created title, and he was only a second lieutenant.

In March 1916, Pancho Villa and several hundred of his bandits raided the town of Columbus, New Mexico, killing a total of seventeen American citizens. Villa's reasoning for this barbaric butchery was that he was angry at the American government because it refused to assist him in his revolution and attempted takeover of the Mexican government. In response to the raid, Gen. John J. Pershing organized a punitive expedition to pursue Villa into Mexico.

Pershing took Patton along as an unofficial aide. Patton led a raid at a place called the Rubio Ranch, believing that one of Villa's men might be there. As it turned out, not one but three of the enemy were there, and during their attempted escape, Patton and his men engaged them in a lively skirmish resembling an old western movie gunfight. All three of the bandits were killed. Patton triumphantly strapped the bodies to the Dodge touring cars used as light transport, one corpse on each hood. He took them directly to Pershing's headquarters for identification, where

General Patton with Gen. Dwight D. Eisenhower in Palermo, Sicily.

General Patton and an aide with entertainers Jack Pepper, Bob Hope, Frances Langford, and Tony Romano.

3

he created quite a commotion. In the Wild West tradition, he carved two notches in his ivory-handled Colt .45 to commemorate his good fortune. After that, Pershing always referred to Patton as his bandit. Patton immediately became a national hero. Newspapers in the United States carried stories about his exploits for a full week before the furor died down. More important, Patton's actions signaled the inauguration of motorized warfare. It was the first time a U.S. Army contingent engaged an enemy using motor vehicles. Although Patton and his men had not fought from the cars as they might have from a tank or armored vehicle, the vehicles were used for transportation instead of horses.

When Pershing assumed command of the American Expeditionary Force (AEF), heading for France in World War I, he decided to take Patton with him. At this time Patton became interested in some new contrivances called tanks. These weren't only new, they were also unreliable, unwieldy, and unproven instruments of warfare. There was a great deal of doubt as to whether or not tanks even had any function or value on the battlefield.

Patton was the first officer assigned to the U.S. Tank Corps. Throwing himself into the job with his usual enthusiasm, he quickly became the AEF's leading tank expert. He almost single-handedly formed the American Tank School. He wrote the training manuals, devised the training regimen and methodologies, and wrote a seminal paper that became the basis for the U.S. Tank Corps doctrine. He taught and trained his tankers and eventually led them into combat.

On the first day of the Meuse-Argonne offensive, Patton was very nearly killed. A bullet struck him in the upper leg and passed completely through him, ripping a large piece of flesh out of his lower buttocks. In spite of his profuse bleeding, he kept advancing until the loss of blood forced him to stop. Luckily, he was evacuated to a rear-echelon hospital before he bled to death on the battlefield. It was the final combat that he would see in

World War I. The armistice was signed on the day that he sneaked out of the hospital to return to his unit. Because of this wound and his great sense of humor, he would occasionally refer to himself as a half-assed general.

After the armistice was signed, Patton returned to the United States as an officer of the Tank Corps. Shortly afterward, he returned to his first love, the cavalry. The reason for his departure from the Tank Corps was the stinginess of the U.S. Congress. After Congress allotted a total of five hundred dollars for a full year of research and development for the Tank Corps, Patton realized that during the years of peace there would be no American development of the tank because of the miserly Congress. As usual, he was correct in his analysis. The development of the tank and armored doctrine stagnated in the United States. It took the events of World War II and the German blitzkrieg to open the eyes of the pacifistic Americans.

In the 1920s and 1930s, Patton was working hard and soldiering very seriously. In addition to his reading and polo playing, he invented a machine-gun sled that could give assault riflemen more direct fire support. He conceived and designed a new saddle pack to increase the range and striking power of cavalry. He worked closely with J. Walter Christie to improve the silhouette, suspension, power, and weapons of tanks. He designed and constructed tank models. He originated plans to restructure infantry divisions into a triangular form, as opposed to the old square formation, to squeeze more maneuverability and firepower out of fewer men.

During this same decade, Patton served in a variety of assignments where he completed his military education. He was an honor graduate of the Command and General Staff College at Fort Leavenworth, Kansas, and a distinguished graduate of the Army War College. In the early 1930s, while stationed at Pearl Harbor, Patton wrote a highly prophetic discussion paper. It dealt with the possibility of an air attack by the Japanese against the

5

Hawaiian Islands. Patton held the firm opinion that Japan had explicit and definite ideas about domination of the Pacific region. His paper outlined almost exactly the plan used by the Japanese on December 7, 1941.

Patton continually sought ways to create more and better mobility in operations. He became an authority on amphibious landings. To better understand airplanes and the role of airpower in war, he obtained a pilot's license and bought and flew his own Stinson airplane. He was one of the first to see the importance and flexibility of employing a light airplane for communications and liaisons. He accomplished all of this on his own before the Japanese attack on Pearl Harbor.

In 1939, Patton was assigned to the 2d Armored Brigade stationed at Fort Benning, Georgia. His skillful management of the 2d Brigade quickly caused him to be given command of the entire 2d Armored Division. He was soon considered to be America's leading tank expert.

In 1942, Patton was assigned the task of creating the Desert Training Corps (DTC) in the Mojave Desert, which spans large parts of California, Nevada, and Arizona. It was at the DTC that modern U.S. tank doctrine and tactics were created and perfected by Patton and his men.

The first contingent of trained tanker units deployed from the DTC as part of Operation Torch, the landing in North Africa. Patton had been instrumental in the detailed planning of the entire amphibious operation, since he was one of the leading American amphibious landing experts in the European theater of operations. The task force sailed from Norfolk, Virginia, and landed on the shores of French Morocco in 1942. It was the first American force to land and fight on foreign soil during World War II.

In the spring of 1943, Patton took command of the II Corps after its disastrous defeat at Kasserine Pass in Tunisia. In his customary fashion, he not only took command, he grabbed it by the throat. He quickly straightened out the disorganized American units, led them to victory at El Guettar, and then turned over command of the corps to his deputy, Omar Bradley.

As commanding general of the Seventh Army in Sicily, Patton stole the glory that General Montgomery so badly wanted. Hampered by higher echelon and sparse supplies, and forced to use secondary roads, Patton and his Seventh Army still reached Messina before Montgomery. Montgomery was surprised and embarrassed to march into the town and find Patton and his men sitting there, waiting for him.

In the spring of 1944, Patton sailed to England on the ocean liner *Queen Mary* to assume command of the U.S. Third Army, his most remembered and most victorious weapon. After the D day landing, Patton and Lucky Forward (Third Army's code name) swept through Europe with a vengeance. Attacking in four directions at once, they drove across France, destroying every German in their path. In December, when the Germans launched the Ardennes offensive (known to Americans as the Battle of the Bulge), Patton's army made a spectacular battle march to relieve the 101st Airborne's Screaming Eagles, who were holding Bastogne against all odds. In the spring of 1945, Patton's army drove relentlessly into Germany, across the Rhine, and into Austria. At the war's end, his soldiers were in Czechoslovakia.

Throughout the war, Patton and his warriors performed magnificently. Third Army had gone farther faster, conquered more territory, and killed, wounded, and captured more enemy soldiers than any other army in the recorded history of war.

Patton died at the age of sixty. The term *age of sixty* is expressly used instead of *sixty years old*. Patton was never old. Men half his age were hard-pressed to keep up with him. He was always the most modern of warriors, always looking for a new, better way to do his job.

Why was George S. Patton Jr. a unique personality? Why should he be considered as an important source of inspiration to today's business managers? Patton was one of the most focused of leaders during his phenomenally successful period as commanding general of the Western Task Force, the Seventh Army, and the Third Army. He spent most of his life studying, training, and preparing himself for his pivotal role in World War II. Anyone who wishes to meet with success in his or her chosen field, be it military or business, has no better role model than General Patton.

IMPORTANT POINTS ABOUT PATTON FOR THE BUSINESS MANAGER

Throughout his career, Patton expended vast amounts of time and energy to learn the intricacies of his chosen profession. Not only was he conversant with the field and technical manuals of his time, he was also familiar with the pages of history, accumulating one of the best military libraries in the world. He understood that history is not just a record of unrelated events. Every act is contiguous—totally dependent upon the previous act. For example, because William the Conqueror defeated Harold at Hastings in 1066, the whole future and history of England was changed. England took a vastly different path than it would have if Harold had been victorious. All of history was thus changed.

Patton recognized this interconnectedness of events for what it is—the basis for all cultural habit, tradition, custom, and the nature of man. The main fascination for Patton in his search for the common elements of man's historical behavior was the significance and importance of military leadership. He continually sought those elusive factors that produce victory or defeat in battle. He was intrigued by the relationships of tactics and supply, maneuver and shock, weapons and willpower.

Patton was anything but a casual reader. He had a habit of making profuse notes in his books, often filling the margins of a page with his own thoughts and concepts. He could lecture extemporaneously on the subjects of scale, chain, armor, German mercenaries, the Italian wars, Polish tactics and techniques, the Peninsular War, and so on, for hours at a time. He wasn't simply cognizant of history; he was familiar and intimate with it: from Greek phalanxes and Roman legions all the way up to and including the mass armies used in World War I (of which he had personal knowledge). He could compare the heavy cavalry of Belisarius with the modern armored vehicle, and he discovered a certain craftiness in the sixth-century tactics of Belisarius that he actually applied to the use of modern tanks.

At the same time, he was thoughtful, contemplative, and circumspect in his analyses of history and war. Unlike intellectuals, he believed that the ultimate virtue in warfare was action. His officers often received lectures on the value, advantage, and benefits of studying history. On numerous occasions, he reported to sick call for the treatment of conjunctivitis, an inflammation of the eyes caused by his many nights of nonstop reading.

Neither was reading the only way Patton gained his military expertise. To him, training was the mucilage that held an army together. Proper training accustomed men to obey orders automatically. Patton knew full well that soldiers on the battlefield could perform their duties only if those duties were second nature to them.

An example of Patton's professional expertise was his use of close support aircraft. Throughout the European campaign of World War II, the XIX Tactical Air Command supported Patton's Third Army. Patton promoted the closest cooperation possible between the air and ground forces. He made sure his ground headquarters and air headquarters were physically located in close proximity. He encouraged a close-knit working atmosphere between the two staffs, going so far as to have them eat their meals together. He constantly applauded the efforts of the airmen and continually directed the attention of newspaper correspondents to the value and importance of air support. He cultivated a feeling of camaraderie, mutual admiration, and cooperation that was beneficial to both the Third Army and the XIX Tactical Air Command.

Patton enjoyed shocking people. He liked to create the impression that he was impulsive in his decisions, acting as though he did everything from instinct. Although it seemed that he had some sort of sixth sense regarding possible enemy action, he was just so imbued with military knowledge, history, and doctrine that everything was already in his mind. All he had to do was to recall it. In Patton's own words, "All the general has to do is retrieve the information from his memory and use the current means at hand to inflict the maximum amount of wounds, death, and destruction on the enemy in the minimum of time." It was this type of knowledge and perception that enabled Patton to deploy his forces confidently with what was incorrectly perceived by some as audacity.

Patton was always loyal to his handpicked staff and appreciated the solid, dependable, and reliable work they performed. They planned well and left little to chance.

Very probably, the best example of Patton's certain grasp on planning occurred in December 1944, when the German Ardennes offensive drove a bulge into the lines of the First Army. Within forty-eight hours, Patton turned his entire Third Army ninety degrees to the north and started a drive that ultimately linked them with the embattled defenders of Bastogne. He threatened the southern flank of the German bulge. The German attack was as good as contained.

Patton held no silly, romantic illusions about warfare. He knew how horrible and hateful war is. He once wrote, "Ever since man banded together with the laudable intention of killing his fellow man, war has been a dirty business." Contrary to popular belief, Patton did not like war. He loathed the chaos, disorder, and destruction of the battlefield. He felt a personal and deep responsibility for the lives of the men in his command. He knew, however, that he must retain a certain detached attitude. The moment he allowed his personal feelings to get in the way, his effectiveness as a general was finished. This was similar to the detachment a doctor must feel while performing surgery on a patient.

Why was Patton so motivated? Why did he have an inclination toward a military way of life? Primarily, it was his only chance for glory, greatness, achievement, fame, and applause, however fleeting they might be. Although he detested the misery, death, and horror of combat, he loved the responsibility and excitement of command. Being exceptionally pragmatic, he viewed himself, his virtue, and his courage as the ultimate weapons of war. In his words, "New weapons are useful in that they add to the repertoire of killing, but, be they tank or tomahawk, weapons are only weapons after all. Wars are fought with weapons, but they are won by Men." Ultimately, what made it possible for Patton to achieve greatness was not just his driving, obsessive willpower. Patton believed in luck. He was lucky enough to have fate on his side. He was the right man, at the right time, and in the right place.

Luck was only a part of it, though. Patton firmly believed that he had been born for the purpose of leading men in a desperate battle for the preservation, the destiny, of his nation. As a believer in reincarnation, he felt that this was his fate—forever. He said as much in his poem, "Through A Glass, Darkly":

> So forever in the future,
> Shall I battle as of yore,
> Dying to be born a fighter,
> But to die again, once more.

Patton's luck, the needs of his nation, and fate all intertwined. When opportunity knocked on his door, Patton was ready and more than willing. He was, in many respects, similar to a diamond—hard, multifaceted, and fascinating to watch. He was essentially a warrior. A man of action, he was also a man of wit, culture, and knowledge. America was lucky to have had him on her side.

11

General Patton bidding farewell to British Gen. Bernard L. Montgomery at the Palermo, Sicily, airport.

General Patton riding the horse Favery Africa, which Adolf Hitler had picked out to be presented to Emperor Hirohito of Japan.

DEMING, SHEWHART, AND STATISTICAL QUALITY CONTROL

American businesspeople are being forced by greater competition, fewer resources, and cheap foreign labor to relearn the statistical quality control methods taught by W. Edwards Deming and Walter A. Shewhart. These are the two men whose methods and teachings were partly responsible for the American manufacturing environment that built the war armaments that won World War II.

William Edwards Deming was born on a Wyoming homestead in 1900. At the age of seventeen he enrolled in the University of Wyoming, graduating in 1921. He remained at the university an extra year for additional mathematics training and in 1924 continued his studies at Yale, where he obtained his doctorate in physics.

In 1927, at the Bell Telephone Laboratories in New York, Deming met Walter A. Shewhart, a statistician for the phone conglomerate. Shewhart had developed mathematical techniques to bring industrial processes into what he called "statistical control." Dr. Shewhart had defined the limits of random variation in any aspect of a worker's task, setting acceptable highs and lows so that any points outside those limits could be detected and the causes studied. He trained workers to perform the charting themselves. This allowed them to gain greater control over their own jobs and permitted them to make adjustments on their own initiative. Deming described Shewhart's genius as "recognizing when to act and when to leave a process alone." Deming began a practice, lasting for several years, of traveling to New York to study with Shewhart. Shewhart's theories of statistical quality control became the basis for Deming's own work.

In 1942, W. Allen Wallis, a Stanford University professor, wrote to Dr. Deming asking if there was some way in which

Stanford could contribute to the war effort. Deming quickly responded with a four-page proposal for teaching the Shewhart methods of statistical quality control (SQC) to engineers, inspectors, and others at companies engaged in wartime production. Deming taught the first ten-day statistical methods course in July 1941. He and his assistants traveled throughout the country, teaching a total of thirty-one thousand students.

Although this book contains only a few references to Dr. Deming's statistical quality control philosophy, based on Dr. Shewhart's original ideas, his beliefs are important enough to be included here for the reader's benefit. The italicized matter is quoted directly from Dr. Deming.

THE FOURTEEN POINTS

1. *Create constancy of purpose toward improvement of product and service,* with the aims of becoming competitive, staying in business, and providing jobs.
2. *Adopt the new philosophy.* We are in a new economic age. Western management must awaken to the challenge, learn its responsibilities, and take on leadership for change.
3. *Cease dependence on mass inspection to achieve quality.* Eliminate the need for inspection on a mass basis by building quality into the product in the first place.
4. *End the practice of awarding business on price tag alone.* Instead, minimize total cost. Move toward a single supplier for any one item, developing a long-term relationship of loyalty and trust.
5. *Improve constantly and forever the system of production and service* to improve quality and productivity and thus constantly decrease costs.
6. *Institute training* on the job.

7. *Institute leadership.* The aim of supervision should be to help people, machines, and gadgets do a better job. Supervision of management is in need of overhaul, as well as supervision of production.
8. *Drive out fear,* so that everyone can work effectively for the company, and employees are not afraid to ask questions or take a position.
9. *Break down barriers between departments.* People in research, design, sales, and production must work as a team to foresee problems in production and use that may be encountered with the product or service.
10. *Eliminate slogans, exhortations, and targets for the workforce* asking for zero defects and new levels of productivity. Such exhortations only create adversarial relationships, as most of the causes of low quality and low productivity belong to the system and thus lie beyond the power of the workforce.
11. *Eliminate numerical quotas.* Substitute leadership.
12. *Remove barriers to pride of workmanship,* abolish the annual merit rating, and eliminate management by objective.
13. *Institute a vigorous program to encourage education, retraining, and self-improvement for everyone.*
14. *Take action to accomplish the transformation* by putting everyone in the company to work on it. The transformation is everybody's job.

THE SEVEN DEADLY DISEASES

1. *The crippling disease: lack of constancy of purpose.*
2. *Emphasis on short-term profits.*
3. *Evaluation by performance, merit rating, or annual review of performance.*
4. *Mobility of management;* i.e., job hopping.

5. *Management by use of visible figures only* (counting the money), with little or no consideration of figures that are unknown or unknowable.
6. *Excessive medical costs.*
7. *Excessive costs of liability, swelled by lawyers who work on contingency fees.*

Note that diseases 6 and 7 are pertinent especially to the United States.

OBSTACLES

1. *Neglect of long-range planning and transformation;* hope for instant pudding.
2. *The supposition that solving problems, automation, gadgets, and new machinery will transform industry.*
3. *The search for examples.* Examples themselves teach nothing. It's necessary to study and know why a practice succeeds or fails.
4. The excuse, *"Our problems are different,"* which is often offered.
5. *Obsolescence in schools,* referring to business schools that teach finance and creative accounting, operating on the theory that management skills can be taught, not learned on the factory floor.
6. *Reliance on quality control departments.*
7. *Blaming the workforce for problems.* Workers are responsible for only 15 percent of problems, the *system* for the other 85 percent. The system is the responsibility of management.
8. Quality by inspection. *You can't inspect quality into a product.*
9. *False starts;* i.e., wholesale teaching of statistical methods to quality control circles whose recommendations are not acted upon by management.

10. *The unmanned computer.* Computers don't fix problems. Often they are merely repositories for unused information.
11. *Meeting specifications.* This is not sufficient if quality and productivity are to improve.
12. *Inadequate testing of prototypes.* What works in the laboratory doesn't necessarily work in production.
13. The attitude that *anyone who comes to try to help us must understand all about our business.* It's possible to know everything about a business except how to improve it and to know how to improve a business without knowing everything about it.

American businesspeople are finally realizing the futility, stupidity, and uselessness of the arrogant manager's attitude that, "I'm the boss, and I know everything You're the employee, and you know nothing." People are beginning to realize that domination and fear don't work when dealing with employees. They are finally beginning to understand the necessity of adopting a businessman-warrior philosophy in response to today's world market.

Precepts used by the military are, have always been, and will always be a good way to conduct business. Professionalism, pragmatism, discipline, and definition and constancy of purpose will never go out of style.

Without a doubt, one man who understood the military way of doing things better than most was Gen. George S. Patton Jr. He also implicitly understood the fact that business and war are very close cousins. His ideas and concepts are as relevant and pertinent in today's world as they were in the 1940s. Moreover, they are relevant to today's complex business community in ways they have never been before. Had Patton chosen business over war as a profession, he would probably have been one of the greatest and most powerful men in the world.

A commander will command.

When you're put in charge—whether it's of an army, division, battalion, company, platoon, or special detail—act like you're in charge. Make damn sure you're in control at all times and that you know what's going on. Ninety percent of being in command is nothing more than making sure orders are followed and the mission is accomplished. Once you've issued an order, get the hell out of the way of the people doing the job, but make sure they know that you're in charge, that you expect them to bring the mission to full fruition, and that they are responsible for its completion.

A good solution applied with vigor now is better than a perfect solution applied ten minutes later.

Nothing is ever going to be perfect, especially during that organized chaos called war. In war a good solution applied now can save lives, materials, and time. You can spend all of your time rethinking and revising your plans and never get the battle started, let alone won. There comes a time when you must simply stop planning and put the plan into effect. If you continue to wait for a perfect plan or for perfect conditions, the enemy will take control of the situation, attack you, force you into a defensive position, and possibly destroy you. Too much analysis causes paralysis.

A pint of sweat will save a gallon of blood.

Soldiers must be trained to such an extent that what they do is second nature to them. The only way to train a soldier is to show him how to do his job and then make him do it over and over. Soldiers must learn to do by doing. They must constantly work at their jobs until their performance becomes a habit so routine, so ingrained in their character, that they can do their jobs in their sleep. There could very well be a time when they might have to function at almost that level of the subconscious. A soldier must be trained and disciplined to such a degree that he won't be bothered by bombs exploding nearby, by strafing aircraft, by being shot at, and by the constant confusion and turmoil of the chaotic battlefield. A soldier must be so well trained that nothing short of death will stop him from fulfilling his mission. If brevity is the soul of wit, then, for the soldier, repetition is the heart of instruction.

Lack of training is one of the greatest problems facing American business today. All too often, management shuns training on the grounds that it's too expensive or that the worker should be working, not wasting company time by being unproductive. When this philosophy controls a company, workers learn their jobs from other workers who were, themselves, poorly trained. They pick up bad habits and they don't fully learn their jobs. When one company's management believes workers can't be spared to learn new methods and new equipment, a competing company that doesn't follow that idiotic line of thought will gain ground. Companies that train their employees will have the advantage, not just in the present, but in the future as well. Technology changes constantly. If American business doesn't change along with technology, it will be doomed to a slow and painful death. Refer to Deming's points 6, *Institute training,* and 13, *Institute a vigorous program to encourage education, retraining, and self-improvement for everyone.*

Any man who thinks he's indispensable, ain't.

To see just how essential you are in the vast scheme of things, put your hand into a bucket of water and look at the hole it leaves when you remove it. No one is indispensable. It's about time the top level of command realized that. It's the job of the commander to lead his soldiers. It's his job to be in the front lines where the shooting is taking place. If you can't accept the responsibility, requirements, and inherent danger of command, get the hell out. A lot of stars on a person's shoulders doesn't mean he is more important; it only means he has a better job.

———————————————

In the business environment, many managers—especially those in the top echelons—hide themselves in their offices, buffer themselves from the workforce with their secretaries, and think that they are too important to mingle with riffraff employees. Many think they're irreplaceable—that the company would immediately cease to function if something happened to them. Actually, the opposite is true. If the board of directors of any large American corporation all died in a plane crash, the company would continue to run simply due to the bureaucracy instilled in it. The employees—the ones who really perform the work necessary to keep the company alive—would continue to function. It would take a very short time to replace the top levels of management, and the new people would at least bring some new ideas with them. The resulting promotions would also be good for the company at all levels.

As long as man exists, there will be war.

Battle is the most magnificent competition in which a man can indulge. Conflict is a basic part of mankind's nature. Conflict, the need for competition, is what makes grown men play games when war is not available. Only those who have the greatest need for conflict will always play their best and hardest to win. Whether it's war, baseball, or business, a winner plays to win and hates to lose. I don't want anyone in my command who loses gracefully. In a game, when a person loses, only the ego is bruised, but in war, and to a great extent in life and business, a whole nation can be lost. There are always those pacifists who will say that everything has changed since the last war and that everything is different now. They say that all we need is a world organization to work together for peace on earth. They have been around for centuries and for those centuries they have signed the death warrants of tens of thousands of people who end up fighting the wars that the pacifists are too cowardly to fight. The pacifist is the worst hypocrite of all. He refuses to fight for and defend that which fights for and defends him—his nation.

As long as there are people on the earth, there will be a need for jobs. Very probably the greatest problem facing American business is the inability of management to understand that making money is not the real reason for being in business. As strange and possibly offensive as that may sound to an American, it's true. The main purpose of business today is to stay in business and to provide jobs for the nation's workers through the use of innovation, research, constant improvement, and equipment maintenance. There is too much emphasis placed on quarterly profits and too little emphasis placed on planning for the next five to ten years. When American businesspeople begin to realize this one fact, they will begin their trek on the road to recovery. Refer to Deming's point 1, *Create constancy of purpose toward improvement of product and service;* deadly diseases 1, *The crippling disease: lack of constancy of purpose,* and 2, *Emphasis on short-term profits;* and obstacle 1, *Neglect of long-range planning and transformation.*

Be alert to the source of trouble.

A good commander will always be fully aware of what's going on in his organization and see trouble before it can stop an advance. This is one of the most important responsibilities of being a commander. Make sure you know where the source of the trouble is as well as the trouble itself. By attacking the source, you stop trouble in its tracks instead of letting the enemy jerk you around and take control by forcing you to attack the trouble spot. Simply put, just make sure you fight the disease and not the symptoms of the disease. The object is not to beat a snake to death but to cut its head off with one quick slice.

By perseverance, study, and eternal desire, any man can become great.

Anyone who is willing to work hard and strive continously to be the best they can possibly be at their chosen profession has the potential to attain the stature of greatness. You must remember that being great doesn't always mean that you will also be notable, rich, or famous. Some people believe, incorrectly, that being great means only that you must have a direct, profound, or monumental impact on history. Many great people have just not lived at exactly the right place and time to be perceived as great. They have not had the luck to be called upon even though they merit the duty that would have placed their name on the honor roll of history. But by their consistency, by their stableness of mind and thought, by their strength of character, and by their focus on goals and objectives, they are great just the same.

In business, management must understand that it must persevere, study, and have an eternal desire to create and sell a quality product. It has no alternative but to constantly strive to improve product, service, and production processes. Management can't just hurry; it must run like hell to keep up with worldwide competitors and to outdo them with better-quality products. It's an unending, never-ceasing situation. Management had better understand and accept that before it is destroyed by the competition. Refer to Deming's point 5, *Improve constantly and forever the system of production and service.*

Do everything you ask of those you command.

There is nothing more disgusting or destructive to morale than officers who do not share dangers and hard conditions with their soldiers. A man who sits on his ass in the comfort of an office while his men are on the front lines facing death, disfigurement, and constant suffering doesn't deserve to be in command of anything. This goes especially for those in the top levels of command—men who think they're so important and indispensable that everything will fall apart if they are killed. These men are arrogant, pompous fools. There's nothing like the death of a top-level officer to cause a much needed round of promotions throughout an army. When I'm asked why I go to the front and take the chances I take, my reply is always, "What the hell good is a commander who won't get shot at?"

Do not fear failure.

No one can be 100 percent correct 100 percent of the time. The best you can do is couple all of the information currently at hand with your past experience and historical knowledge to make the best decision at any given moment. Even when you do fail (and you will) it's an excellent learning experience. At least you will know what not to do in a specific situation. If you fear failure, you will never be able to make a difficult decision that may require a calculated risk. By fearing failure, you prepare yourself to become one of those cautious people who tries to win by not losing. If you're afraid of failing, you will never achieve true success or win a decisive victory. Only people who never do anything make no mistakes. That's the greatest mistake of all.

Do not make excuses, whether it's your fault or not.

Do what you think is right and don't apologize for it. You don't need to defend or justify either yourself or your decisions. If your actions don't achieve your goal, admit it, file the experience in your memory, and continue with your plan of action. Persevere! Very often, it's the commander who keeps slugging away who wins the battle. Don't expect life to be fair and luck to be always on your side. Your abilities must make up for bad luck and unfair situations. Admit your mistakes, learn from them, and focus on the next battle.

Do not take counsel of your fears.

Although this may seem like a repeat of the "do not fear failure" maxim, it's vastly different in meaning and context. What this means is not to let your fears dictate your actions. If you fear that something might happen and you react to that fear and plan according to it, you are letting the fear control your actions and write your orders. At that point, you are no longer in control. Fear has taken control, and fear will make you do many stupid, irresponsible, and foolish things. If, however, you don't take counsel of your fears, you can make your own plans according to your own goals and objectives. Don't let yourself be fooled into fighting against fear instead of fighting against the enemy.

In the business community, it's fundamentally imperative that management not run a business based on fear and intimidation. In many cases, when employees are fearful of retribution by management, they refuse to ask questions or offer suggestions. Very often they continue to do their job incorrectly instead of asking for help and they won't tell management when problems arise for fear of being blamed. Employees must feel secure in their jobs before they can be outspoken about problems. They should be part of the process, not afraid of the process. Refer to Deming's point 8, *Drive out fear.*

Do your duty as you see it and damn the consequences.

Before you'll be able to do this, you'll have to possess moral courage. Probably the greatest failing there is in a commander is lack of moral courage. You must be your own person, be able to make your own decisions, and have the guts to stand by those decisions. If you can't do it, you don't deserve the responsibility of command. Commanders lacking moral courage are nothing less than potential murderers.

Every leader must have the authority to match his responsibility.

There is no way a man can accomplish any mission if he hasn't been given the full authority necessary to make things happen. An equally detrimental situation is for higher command to second-guess subordinates. If a man doesn't receive adequate authority or is always being questioned or counseled by his bosses, he will eventually stop doing anything. Why should he bother when he will be second-guessed and his orders have no real power anyway? The frustration of such a situation will erode the average man's self-confidence and self-motivation. The man in the field is the one who really knows what is going on—what the current conditions are. He's the only one who can react quickly enough to rectify errors and exploit opportunities. When you give a man an assignment, leave him alone. Let him make his own decisions, give him the power to perform his job, and stay the hell out of his way. If you don't like the way he is doing the job, either relieve him and put someone else in charge or do it yourself. Most people will surprise you with their motivation, ingenuity, and determination.

General Patton praises his troops for the job they have been doing.

Genius comes from the ability to pay attention
to the smallest detail.

Unsuccessful commanders issue orders and then return to their card games at headquarters. They believe the simple act of issuing an order will immediately cause everything to fall into place, and the battle will go their way just because they said so. They expect everything to go exactly according to their plans. That is as unrealistic as it is stupid. A successful commander issues an order and then makes damn sure it's not only carried out but working as planned. If things go wrong, or if a situation changes, the commander will be aware of it immediately and be able to change the orders in response to the current situation. When necessary, verbal orders will override written orders to make sure things get done quickly. When issuing verbal orders, make it obligatory that your subordinates repeat the orders back to you to make sure they fully understand them. Don't jump to conclusions and don't make assumptions. Follow up on everything.

Give credit where it's due.

This actually means two things. First, it means to tell someone when he's done a good job. Praise him for his performance and give him credit for being a good soldier. Make sure other people know he's doing a good job and that the praise gets into his personnel folder. It takes very little time to do this, and it reaps great rewards. Second, giving credit where it's due means not being so stupid as to take credit for what your soldiers do. There are people who will listen to a soldier's ideas, say they are no good, and then claim them as their own. These people are galling enough, but even worse are those who realize that a soldier is doing good work and has some good ideas and try to get in on it. They will try to involve themselves in the soldier's work with the intention of stealing the work and the credit for it. Usually these dishonest schemers outrank their victims. They think their theft will be protected by the chasm of rank. To thwart these thieves, you should keep a diary. Write all your ideas and thoughts in it, including dates and times. This may not protect your ideas from being stolen, but it will at least document the fact that they were originally yours.

Good tactics can save even the worst strategy.
Bad tactics will destroy even the best strategy.

It's not the high-ranking commanders at the top levels who win battles; it's the soldier in the field who either wins or loses. Anyone with average intelligence can come up with a decent strategy, but the tactical offensive is what wins a battle, and the soldier in the field is the final tactical tool of war. The problem is that if the soldiers don't have the proper equipment, food, and fighting spirit, they will fail in their mission. It's the responsibility of the top ranks to support the soldiers, to keep them adequately supplied, and to motivate them to the high levels of morale and devotion to duty required of a winning team. If the top ranks don't properly support the field soldier, tactical losses will be assured. Any top-level commander with adequate training can devise large-scale strategy. At that level, they are really no longer warriors or commanders; they are nothing more than office managers. The bottom line is that it's the soldier in the field who will be either victorious or defeated.

Haste and speed are not synonymous.

Do not confuse them. Speed means that properly planned actions executed rapidly have a great chance of success. Haste means that poorly or improperly planned actions will probably fail— and badly. Hastily planned actions will be doomed to failure, causing the loss of lives, materials, and especially that most important element of combat, time. Operations must be handled as quickly as possible at all times, but not at the risk of being hasty. Things must be done right the first time. There won't be a second chance.

In business production, haste must be viewed as a numerical quota, while speed may be viewed as quality output. With numerical quotas, workers are forced to manufacture defective products. By the time the quota has been met, the product is already defective. The product must be either scrapped or reworked. Scrapping means a complete waste of materials and production time. Reworking means a further waste of time and manpower. Had the product been manufactured correctly the first time, even if it took longer without a quota, the savings would have been dramatic. Doing it right the first time means no waste of raw materials or production time and no loss of pride of workmanship. Refer to Deming's point 11, *Eliminate numerical quotas.*

I prefer a loyal staff officer to a brilliant one.

Loyalty is one of the most important links in the chain of command. It is absolutely imperative for successful military operations. Loyalty must be a two-way street—from the top down and from the bottom up. A loyal staff officer will do more, do it better, and do it without complaint. Brilliant staff officers will invariably let their egos get in the way of doing a good job for the team. They're troublesome and self-centered and they're more interested in their own careers than they are in following orders and winning as team members.

I reread Freeman's Norman Conquest, paying particular attention to the roads used by William the Conqueror during his operations in Normandy and Brittany. The roads used in those days had to be on ground which was always practical.

In modern war, the first things a retreating enemy will destroy are roads and railways. By knowing what type of ground is practical for use as temporary or impromptu roads, troops can maneuver more easily. By knowing the history of a battleground, a commander can save a lot of time when it's necessary to bypass damaged roads instead of having to repair them. In short, use what you know works—stick to the basics. Don't reinvent the wheel, experiment, or try unproved theories. It only wastes valuable time you don't have and causes problems. Any good football coach will tell you that a team can never win if they don't know and practice the basics of the game. Elaborate and flamboyant plays are useless if your team can't master the fundamentals of blocking and tackling.

If a man has done his best, what else is there?

Always do your best no matter what job you have to do. Never do less than you can with the skills, tools, and abilities you have at your disposal. After all is said and done, let history be your judge. Above all, never criticize yourself—you'll find there are always more than enough people who will gladly do it for you. Unless you do your best, the day will come when, tired and hungry, you will halt just short of the goal you were ordered to reach, and by halting, you will make useless the efforts and deaths of thousands.

In case of doubt, attack.

The enemy is just as ignorant of the situation as you are and perhaps more so. Instead of waiting to see what might develop, attack constantly, vigorously, and viciously. If you're standing around trying to figure out what is happening or what the enemy is up to, you are making one hell of a good target out of yourself and your men. Never let up. Never stop. Always attack. When the enemy is defending himself against your assault, he doesn't have the time to plan an offensive against you. If you were a boxer and your opponent were on the ropes, you wouldn't stop and let him rest, would you? When you get him on the ropes, keep punching. Beat the hell out of him until he's out for the count. *"L'audace, l'audace, toujours l'audace."*

In the long run, it's what we do, not what we say, that will destroy us.

This is particularly pertinent to the generally oleaginous politicians running our government. They'll say anything to get elected. Once elected, however, they rarely, if ever, do anything they said. It's bad enough when politicians do this but worse yet when soldiers do it. The unfortunate truth is that real soldiers, those with a true warrior spirit, are ignored, pushed aside, and never promoted to high rank because of their inherently pugnacious nature. It's the political soldiers (actually politicians in uniform) who will be anointed with the mantle of high command—all because they say what the civilian politicians want to hear and will slavishly follow any order no matter how detrimental it might be to the moral fabric of the nation.

Business, too, has its slick political types who care little for a company, its employees, or the quality of its products. These people must be confronted at every opportunity to expose their true stripe. When discovered, they should be removed by upper management as quickly as possible. In today's environment of hostile takeovers and greenmail, these scoundrels will do anything to benefit themselves. Although they will say anything to get what they want—including lies and half-truths—it's their actions that demonstrate their true purpose. When you encounter these people, keep minutes of all meetings and write reports comparing what they say with what they do. Use this evidence to frustrate and halt their schemes. The first time their actions are contrary to their rhetoric they become suspect. From then on, they must be watched.

It seems very strange to me that we invariably entrust the writing of our regulations for the next war to men totally devoid of anything but theoretical knowledge.

There are, of course, a number of reasons for this stupidity. The men who do the actual fighting in wartime are very often killed during combat. Dead men have no opinions. Those combat veterans who do survive the rigors of battle are normally neither bookish nor scholarly by nature. Therefore, they are ignored by the higher level of commands populated by intellectuals who run the service schools. Combat veterans are very often less than appreciated during peacetime, being considered belligerent, troublesome, and lacking in the social graces valued by the politically oriented high command. Thus they are never considered politically qualified for higher rank. One major reason for this situation is the self-serving politicians and civilians in charge of the services. These political hacks want only soldiers who will not question orders, no matter how destructive they are to the military community. The politicians who run the military are interested only in paying off political debts; they are not interested in preserving the military forces that protect the nation.

In the business world, this clique mentality precludes capable and qualified individuals from advancement. Many excuses are used; few are relevant. I know secretaries who have literally trained new bosses to do their jobs. Why wasn't the secretary promoted? I know men in management positions who require such stringent qualifications for subordinates that they, themselves, wouldn't be qualified for the job. These tactics are used for no other purpose than to allow the managers to hire or promote either sycophants or those who fit into a nonthreatening mold.

48

It's better to fight for something in life than to die for nothing.

The fact is, and statistics prove it, three out of three people die. There are no two-hundred-year-old people on the earth, and very few live to be one hundred. For that matter, very few do anything of note after reaching the age of sixty. Since you already know that you're destined to die, why not live your life with some purpose in mind? It's better to die for a just and honorable cause at a young age than to die in bed from the withering effects of old age.

In business, of course, people don't die at the hands of the competitors. However, sometimes they are demoted or fired. The point is that if you're going to be punished or fired for speaking your mind, you might as well do a good job of it. The cause should be an employee wanting to do the best job possible to produce a quality product and not failing to let management know their opinion. Why do people wait until they're quitting or retiring from a job to tell the exit interviewer what they really think about what's going on in a company? It's as much the employee's responsibility to inform management about problems as it is management's responsibility to act on the employee's information and suggestions. For that reason, no employee should be afraid to tell it like it is—to let their boss know what they feel about things. Refer to Deming's points 8, *Drive out fear,* and 14, *Take action to accomplish the transformation.*

49

It's really amazing what . . . determination on the part of one man can do to many thousands.

Simply by being determined, a man can instill courage, confidence, and discipline in his soldiers. With determination a person can link leadership and confidence to create an image of ability and brilliance. People want to be associated with other people who are determined and confident. They want to be associated with a winner. If you can give the impression of being a winner, of being imbued with the determination to never quit, to never let the notion of losing enter into your thoughts, people will follow. By giving the impression of being determined, you can cause people to act like winners, and they can become what they aspire to be—winners. It follows like the links in a chain that if you are determined to think like a winner, act like a winner, talk like a winner, and be like a winner, you will be a winner.

General Patton holding a giant shotgun in front of his headquarters in Germany.

***It's the unconquerable soul of man,
and not the nature of the weapon he uses,
that ensures victory.***

Many misinformed, ignorant, and ill-educated people believe that some new or magic weapon can always be used to win battles and wars. The same thought followed the development of dynamite, the Gatling gun, gunpowder, the bow and arrow, and even the much ballyhooed atom bomb. I fear that future leaders will be lulled into a false sense of security by thinking that weapons like the A-bomb are so magical that we will never again have to fight a war. It's just this type of illogical pacifistic idiocy that will cause us to be pecked to death by ducks. It's this type of thinking that makes ignorant people believe that success in war may be attained by the use of some wonderful invention rather than by hard fighting and superior leadership. War is an art and as such is not susceptible to explanation by fixed formulas.

In the business world, it's the computer that has become the theoretical savior of mankind. The problem is that, in the same stupid way that government throws money at a problem, business throws a computer at a problem. Computers and other technological gadgets are only tools. If used correctly, they can be of some value, but they will never replace good planning and hard work to produce a quality product. In a great many cases, computers house incredible masses of information that will never be used. A shovel can't dig a hole; why expect a computer to solve a problem? Refer to Deming's obstacle 2, *The supposition that solving problems, automation, gadgets, and new machinery will transform industry.*

Keep a quick line of communications.

When people need to discuss things with you, they shouldn't be filtered through a bunch of other people to see you. A sure sign that a commanding officer thinks too highly of himself is that he will buffer himself with levels of hierarchy. These people begin to believe they're too important to talk to anyone. They begin to believe that their time is too valuable to be wasted on people other than their superiors and their own pet projects. When this happens, the commander becomes isolated. He loses touch with his soldiers and accordingly loses all knowledge and perception of his command. The most dangerous thing that happens, though, is that his chief of staff becomes the most powerful man in the organization, being able to decide who can and cannot talk to the commanding officer, what is important to be discussed at meetings, and who will and will not get their ideas presented to the commanding officer. A very quick and easy way to keep this from happening is to simply answer your own phone. People will be surprised as hell when they contact you directly with one phone call. They'll also appreciate it. Just keep the calls brief and to the point.

Know what you know and know what you don't know.

This is not as peculiar as it may sound. It means you have certain information available from a number of sources, such as your intelligence officer, daily activity reports, unit operation reports, and past experience. There are numerous things you don't know, such as exactly what the weather will be like when you attack, exactly where and when the enemy might stage an attack or counterattack, whether the enemy is demoralized and will offer light resistance, and whether or not the citizens of the town you're attacking are sympathetic or frightened and might wish to surrender in spite of the enemy soldiers entrenched there. You can even use unknown information to your advantage. A good example of unknown information is the radio silence imposed on units by the German command during the buildup for the Battle of the Bulge. Although we had no specific knowledge of what was being planned or what was going to happen, we knew from past experience that radio silence meant something was going to happen very soon. By adding this information to what we did know, our G2 (Intelligence) assessed the situation, calculated the possibilities, and came to the conclusion that the Germans would, in fact, attack. The offensive initiated by the Germans was almost exactly what our G2 people had predicted. The unfortunate part was that SHAEF (Supreme Headquarters Allied Expeditionary Forces) ignored our warnings and let it happen. As soon as you learn something that you didn't know before, add it to your store of known information. Keep your information current. Information is like an egg, the fresher, the better. Don't jump to conclusions, and don't make assumptions.

Lack of orders is no excuse for inaction.

It's everyone's job to strive unceasingly toward goals and objectives to ensure total victory. Don't think that you're finished just because you've reached one objective. Don't wait for orders to continue the battle. While you're working and fighting for the current objective, you must be planning for the next assault. History is full of tragic accounts of campaigns lost because leaders stopped on the wrong side of a river, because they didn't have the initiative to exploit the advantage of a battle just won, and because they failed to obey the basic requirement to constantly be on the offensive. I assure all of my officers and soldiers that I have never and will never criticize them for having done too much. However, I shall certainly relieve them for doing nothing. When orders fail to come they must act on their own best judgment. A very safe rule to follow is that in case of doubt, push on a little farther and then keep on pushing.

Like wine, accounts of valor mellow with age; until Achilles, dead 3,000 years, stands peerless.

This may also be referred to as the Eisenhower Syndrome. Like the cliché that the grass is greener on the other side, this philosophy misleads commanders to lack trust in people they know. The susceptible commander believes that someone, usually an unknown personality, is better than his own people, that some expert from somewhere else will perform miracles where his own people cannot. All of the ancient heroes and warrior-kings were only men. They were not gods with superhuman strength, intelligence, and wisdom. It's the historian who imbues these ancients with such omnipotence and omniscience. There are men in our ranks today who could well have been great historical figures if they had lived thousands of years ago. On the other hand, Julius Caesar would have a hell of a time being a brigadier general in my army. Anyone sufficiently remote in time and distance can be perceived as more than they really are. This was one of the great failings of Ike. He often perceived officers in other theaters of operation as being better than those in his own command. Because he knew these latter personally and worked with them, he failed to appreciate how good they really were. His intimacy with them often caused him to falsely believe that they were less capable than they were. It was a simple case of familiarity breeding, if not contempt, at least a low opinion of his people.

***Make the mind command the body,
never let the body command the mind.***

Life is filled with pain, both mental and physical. There's not a damn thing you can do about it. If you let your body rule your life, you'll never accomplish anything. When you're tired, when you're sore, when you're sick, when you think you can't go even one more step, that's the time to let the mind take over. The body is merely a shell that must do what the mind orders. As Kipling wrote:

> If you can fill the unforgiving minute
> With sixty seconds' worth of distance run,
> Yours is the Earth and everything that's in it,
> And—which is more—you'll be a Man, my son!

If you're in pain, that's too bad. You might as well be in pain and accomplish something. You'll get plenty of rest after you die.

Make your plans to fit the circumstances.

You can't make your circumstances fit your plans: war is nothing short of organized chaos. Because situations change from day to day, hour to hour, and minute to minute, it's downright stupid (and possibly criminal) to stick to plans that were conceived before the change. One of the reasons we defeated the Germans is because they couldn't think on their feet. They stubbornly and stupidly followed the orders of their superiors, even when they knew those orders were incorrect in light of a changed situation. Our soldiers don't act like that. If necessary, they will improvise on the spur of the moment to take advantage of any situation that offers itself. They will exploit breakthroughs even if plans haven't been designed to incorporate those breakthroughs. Instill in your soldiers the characteristics of self-motivation and self-initiative. When I was in World War I, I instructed a staff officer to change a set of orders to include the use of a smoke screen because of some information I had recently learned. He refused, saying, "The stencil has already been cut." That is the height of stupidity and inflexibility. He was perfectly willing to let men die, if necessary, just so he wouldn't have to retype a stencil.

Many soldiers are led to faulty ideas of war by knowing too much about too little.

In short, beware of the specialist and the expert. The specialist generally sees things from a single viewpoint, his own. Specialists and experts are never cognizant of the full spectrum of light that must shine on a subject or problem before all sides can be viewed circumspectly. They generally lack full knowledge of the big picture. Their opinions and input must be viewed as only partial information. Each specialist—the aviator, the artilleryman, and the tanker—talks as if his was the only useful weapon, and if only enough of them were used, the war would soon end. The simple fact is, it's the soldier in the field, in the final analysis, who does the trick.

In business, the soldier in the field is the worker who actually produces something. It's the newspaper columnist who writes the words, the mechanic who changes spark plugs and oil, the secretary who types (and corrects) the boss's letters, and the sewing machine operator who assembles fabric into clothing. These are the ones who create products to sell. Managers create nothing; it's their job to provide the materials, the equipment, and the environment necessary for the worker to create a product. Managers are responsible for the system, which is responsible for 85 percent of the problems encountered by the workers. Refer to Deming's obstacle 7, *Blaming the workforce for problems.*

Moral courage is the most valuable and usually the most absent characteristic in men.

I cannot count the times I've seen men who should know better than to keep quiet when unjust decisions are being made, decisions that literally affect the lives of tens of thousands of soldiers. These decisions are made, not on the basis of sound military policy, but purely to further the political and personal ambition of officers in high command. Cowardice on the battlefield is disgusting enough. Cowardice in the military planning room is repugnant. It ultimately means the unnecessary death, mutilation, and disfigurement of soldiers for the sake of the commanders. It takes courage to stand up for what is believed to be right and just. Most men seem to lack such courage. Sycophancy for the sake of career is just as deadly as incompetence.

For a business application, see the Patton quote, "It's better to fight for something in life than to die for nothing." Also see Deming's points 8, *Drive out fear,* and 14, *Take action to accomplish the transformation.*

Never fight a battle when nothing is gained by winning.

A Pyrrhic victory is no victory. There must be a valid reason, a purpose for battle, a qualified objective to be gained before submitting your soldiers to combat. It's bad enough to fight and lose. It's even worse to fight and win for no purpose. It borders on criminal negligence. It's equivalent to the murder of your soldiers, and it's a waste of material, supplies, and time.

Never let the enemy pick the battle site.

If you allow the enemy to pick the battle site, you can bet your ass that you won't have a good chance of winning. You'll be playing his game on his terms and fitting right into his plans. If the enemy tries to engage you in a frontal attack, don't let him snare you. Go around him. Get to his rear, attack his headquarters, sever his communications centers, and destroy his supply lines. Cut off the head and you can inflict any destruction you want on the body. Grab him by the nose and kick him in the ass.

Never make a decision too early or too late.

Don't jump to conclusions, don't make assumptions, and don't make hasty decisions. Make sure you have enough information to make a good decision, but don't wait for every scrap of information before you decide, either. Waiting too long to make a choice will allow many an opportunity to be lost. A large part of the decision-making process depends not only on the information you possess about the enemy, his movements, and his capabilities, but also on your past experience and knowledge. I, personally, have often been accused of making hasty and rash decisions. Those are totally incorrect charges made by jealous individuals. I've studied war for decades and I know how an enemy will act and react. Because of my intense study of history, I have a countermove for every move the enemy might make. A good analogy would be to compare the successful commander to a highly qualified surgeon. During surgery, if emergencies arise, the competent and qualified doctor will make immediate decisions depending on exactly what is happening at the moment and do what is necessary to rectify the situation. For this he is called a skilled surgeon. The successful commander will do the same thing during combat to ensure victory with the least loss of life and materials.

Never stop until you have gained the top or the grave.

A person must never stop studying, thinking, working, learning, and doing. Every time you do something wrong, you learn from it. Every time you do something right, you gain confidence and insight. You must never lose your ambition to be better than you are—to be great. Someone has to be on the top, and there's no reason why it can't be you.

No good decision was ever made in a swivel chair.

Get off your ass and out of your office. You can't expect to know what's going on if you spend all your time behind a desk. The only way to know what is happening at any given moment is to see for yourself. Don't rely entirely on reports and secondhand information, no matter how good your staff is. Information, suggestions, and insights from your staff are extremely valuable and should be used to the fullest advantage, but nothing matches personal, first-hand knowledge. When you go to the front, you get to meet the soldiers who are performing the real job of an army and, more important, they get to see you. They'll know you care enough about winning and about them to take the same chances they take every day. Not only will it build your confidence, but it will do wonders for your reputation as a leader. The inspiration of your soldiers does not come by way of coded messages from the safety of a comfortable rear-echelon headquarters office; it comes from the visible, living personality of the leader at the front of the charge. It's the commander's job to know exactly what is happening at all times, and you can't see your organization, meet your people, and gather personal knowledge from inside your office.

Managers, especially those at the top levels, should occasionally get out of their cushy ivory towers and see what is happening in the real world. They don't have to snoop around or stick their noses into the employees' jobs, but they should be seen, and they should be recognizable to the workforce. Most employees wouldn't know the top man or woman in an organization if they saw him or her. It sure as hell wouldn't hurt for the manager to know some of the employees by name, either. Refer to Deming's point 9, *Break down barriers between departments.*

Nothing is ever done twice.

Everything is a final heat. Never think that what you are doing is only in preparation for doing the same thing more fully or better the next time. There is no next time. This is of special application to war. There is only one chance to win a battle. It must be won the first time. You'll never have a second chance. You'll probably be dead.

General Patton urinating in the Rhine River as he had promised to do.
Photo from the author's collection.

Officers must assert themselves by example and by voice.

Speak up—make yourself heard. If you expect your soldiers to act bravely, you'd better act bravely yourself. If you expect your men to dress, act, and think like soldiers, you'd better dress, act, and think like one yourself. You can't be just a good soldier; you must be a better soldier than every one of your subordinates. If you're not the best damn soldier in your unit, you shouldn't be in charge. You must be able to do everything your soldiers do, and you must do it better than any of them. Excuses are unacceptable.

One must choose a system and stick to it.

If you choose to be one of the boys, so be it. If you choose to be an ill-tempered, mean son of a bitch, that's your decision. If you choose to be somewhere in the middle, it's up to you. The main point is to decide on a system that works for you and stay with it while always focusing on the completion of the mission. If you bounce around between command styles, you'll end up doing nothing but confusing your people. By displaying conflicting and bewildering signals to them, you will probably lose their respect. In my opinion, the best commander is the obtrusive and ubiquitous type. You should never forget that it's OK to start out as an asshole and turn into a nice guy, but you must never start out as a nice guy and turn into an asshole. It sounds peculiar, but it derives from human nature. If you change from a nice guy to an asshole, your people will despise you and blame you for all sorts of terrible things, whether they're your fault or not. On the other hand, if you change from an asshole to a nice guy, your people will remember what you can be like if you have to. They'll know what to expect if they don't perform to the best of their ability. They'll know that as long as they do their duty and accomplish their assigned missions, you will generally let them go about their business; but if they slack off or bungle a task, they can most assuredly expect the full force of your unholy wrath to envelop them. At times like this, a well-planned temper is very useful.

Say what you mean and mean what you say.

Don't beat around the bush. Don't use euphemisms and don't speak in glittering generalities (as many of our higher-level commanders do). Choose your words carefully and economically. Be brief and to the point. There is nothing wrong or impolite about succinct orders. Too many words and ambiguous words only confuse an issue. Your soldiers must understand precisely what is expected of them. There must be no confusion when lives and victory are at stake. You should say exactly what you mean and at all times mean exactly what you say. This is of particular importance when it comes to praising soldiers for excellent performance and disciplining them for poor performance. If you tell an officer he will be relieved for incompetence or poor performance, you'd damn well better do it and do it promptly. Punishment for mistakes must be immediate. Failure to adhere to verbal promises will destroy your credibility. The dismal and disgusting conditions in our legal system are an excellent example of what can happen when this concept is neither understood nor followed.

Select leaders for accomplishment and not for affection.

Watch your people closely and keep tabs on them, but do so privately. The winners must always be given the most important assignments. Those who consistently fail to accomplish their tasks and missions should be either relieved or relegated to rear-echelon duties. Victory in combat is too important to be left to someone whose only credentials are that he is your friend. The better people perform, the more authority and responsibility they must be given—along with the most difficult jobs—no matter what you think of them on a personal level. Results are what count, not friendship.

Since the necessary limitations of map problems inhibit the student from considering the effects of hunger, emotion, personality, fatigue, leadership, and many other imponderable yet vital factors, he first neglects and then forgets them.

Nothing teaches as well as personal experience. Soldiers must learn to do by doing. Classroom education is fundamentally a good thing, but it must not be thought of as the supreme learning environment. Just because a student receives a high classroom score doesn't mean he'll make a good commander, let alone a good soldier. Classroom material does nothing more than give you a general idea of what to expect in actual combat. The only way to really learn how to fight is to get involved in a full-scale life-and-death struggle. Nothing can give you combat experience except combat experience. That's an important reason to choose combat veterans for high command and for training roles. Political officers must be kept behind desks where they belong.

The business community must begin to realize that our school system is more than inadequate; it's obsolete. Of course, the teachers' unions will dispute this fact. This predicament can be seen in colleges and at the national political level. In the first situation, college professors who have never owned or run a business are teaching young people how to be managers. In the second situation, college professors who have never dealt in anything other than theory are picked by U.S. presidents to set the tone and direction of government involvement in our school systems. Look where that's gotten us. Management skills cannot be taught; they must be learned in a working environment. Students must learn to do by doing. Refer to Deming's obstacle 5, *Obsolescence in schools.*

Strategy and tactics do not change. Only the means of applying them are different.

Strategy is very simple. It should be used like a steamroller—make up your mind on a course and direction of action and then stick to it. It takes very little imagination and skill to conceive a workable method of strategy. Tactics, however, must not be used in steamroller fashion. Tactics must be applied by attacking weakness and exploiting breakthroughs. This worked for Stone Age men throwing rocks at each other, and it still works in today's advanced technological world. There is an ancient French saying, *"Plus ça change, plus c'est la même chose,"* which means, the more things change, the more they stay the same. Mankind has changed very little during its entire history on this planet. People still get frightened in battle; they still get hungry, suffer from the cold, and die from wounds. If you do enough reading and study enough history, you will discover that what new generations think of as modern concepts and novel ideas were thought of many thousands of years ago by our ancestors. The only thing that has changed is the technology. This ranges from the printing of books, containing philosophies for the improvement of man, to the creation of highly advanced weapons used to inflict wounds and death on an enemy who disagrees with a nation's philosophies. There is nothing new under the sun, only advanced technological methods.

Success is how you bounce on the bottom.

Life is never fair, and it never turns out exactly according to your plans. During a person's lifetime, there is no way to avoid problems, mishaps, and failure. Everyone experiences personal and professional setbacks, difficulties, and obstacles. These hindrances are unimportant, though, except as learning opportunities. What is important is how you react to them. If you want to feel sorry for yourself and give up, that's your prerogative. You always have the option to be a failure. If you want to be successful, however, accept these difficulties, learn from them, put your past behind you, and get on with your life and career. It takes personal strength of character and resilience to focus yourself and continue toward your objectives in spite of the nasty little hurdles and barriers life puts in your pathway. If you really want something badly enough, nothing will stop you from getting it.

Take calculated risks.

The key word here is *calculated*. Almost everything in life is a risk to some degree, especially the outcome of a battle. If you have well-trained soldiers, you have a good chance of winning even though the odds may not be in your favor. The key to a calculated risk lies in the esprit de corps of your soldiers. If you and your enemy have a parity of resources in weapons, supplies, and men, the purely statistical chances of winning will be fifty-fifty. However, if your men are well trained, are highly motivated, have good morale, and possess a fighting and winning spirit, they'll have what it takes to tip the scales and make the fight ninety-ten in your favor. You'll most probably win. Your soldiers' good morale and winning attitude can allow you to take a calculated risk.

The duties of an officer are the safety, honor, and welfare of your country first; the honor, welfare, and comfort of the men in your command second; and the officer's own ease, comfort, and safety last.

This concept should be tattooed on the foreheads of many high-ranking officers, especially some of those at the top levels of command. By giving themselves special privileges and expecting extra consideration, they undermine the structure of loyalty that builds the respect and confidence of their subordinates. Rank may have some privileges during peacetime, but in war special privileges for higher echelons are as dangerous as an enemy's bullet. After the mission, the care, feeding, welfare, and comfort of the soldier in the field are the most important considerations.

Here's one to chew on. How often do you think a CEO or high-level manager thinks about employees as anything other than an expense item eating away at his profits? Managers easily forget that the reason for being in business shouldn't be just to make money; it should be to stay in business and provide jobs. This is a key point. Management (for the most part) is totally and absolutely backward in its perceptions of workers and business. Management's normal response to problems and poor-quality products is to blame the worker. Workers are responsible for approximately 15 percent of all problems. The system is responsible for the other 85 percent. The system is the responsibility of management. Refer to Deming's obstacle 7, *Blaming the workforce for problems.*

The leader must be an actor.

The simple act of wearing a uniform doesn't make a man a leader or a warrior. Many of our top leaders look and act like anything but the death-dealing warriors they are supposed to be. The leader is unconvincing unless he lives the part of a warrior. By living the role completely, he becomes what he aspires to be. He must eat, sleep, and live war. He must never stop striving to attain the elusive warrior spirit, the vitalizing spark that ignites the soul to heights of courage and triumph. No one is born a leader or a warrior. Some people are, without doubt, born with superior personal attributes, attributes that are conducive to the warrior's development. Few are born in the mold of a warrior. However, the question of whether or not a man can learn to be a warrior is answerable in the affirmative. There is considerable truth in the age-old adage that as a man thinketh, so is he. If a man has the fixed determination to acquire the warrior soul and, having acquired it, lives by the philosophy of either conquering or perishing with honor, he will have achieved his goal. A man of diffident manner will never inspire confidence. A cold reserve cannot beget enthusiasm.

General Patton discusses the situation in Sicily with Brig. Gen. Theodore Roosevelt Jr.

The more senior the officer, the more time he has to go to the front.

Very few high-ranking officers will ever admit it, but the higher you are in rank, the less you have to do. An army's work is done primarily at the platoon and company level. Instead of getting waffle ass[1] and feeling important, a commander must see to it that his army is constantly moving forward and that all of his soldiers are fully employed at all times. Commanding an army is not such an absorbing task, with the exception that the commander must be ready at all hours of the day and night to make some momentous decision. Often those momentous decisions are nothing more than frequently having to tell somebody who thinks he is beaten that he is not.

1. Waffle ass is a curable condition in which a manager's buttocks are imprinted with the seat design of his chair due to infrequent periods of movement.

The great things a man does appear to be great
only after they are done.
When they're at hand, they are normal decisions
and are done without knowledge
of their greatness.

It's impossible to predict a great victory. Even the greatest paint-
ers and composers were unable to say, "Today I am going to create a masterpiece." It just doesn't happen that way. It's for exactly that reason that people must always be cognizant of what
they are doing and why they are doing it. If you continuously focus on an objective and never stop thinking about it, aiming for
it, and working toward it, every decision you make will be for
the purpose of that ultimate goal. Only when the goal is eventually attained will you be able to look back and objectively assess
your performance and all of the decisions you made during the
campaign. Only then will you be able to analyze your decisions
and determine which ones were insignificant, which ones were
adequate, and which ones were absolutely brilliant. Hindsight is
the only method by which you can view your history correctly
and ascertain its proper perspective. Only after the fact will you
be able to see which decisions were truly momentous, acutely
imperative, and crucial to victory.

The soldier is the army.

No army is better than the soldiers in it. To be a good soldier, a man must have discipline, self-confidence, self-respect, pride in his unit, and pride in his country. He must have a high sense of duty and obligation to his comrades and to his superiors. None of this can happen if the leaders at the top levels and the commanding officers of individual units are self-serving, if they are not dedicated to the soldiers in the field. Don't forget what it was like when you were just starting out. A little consideration isn't going to kill you. As you rise in rank, remember this. Instill the concepts of loyalty, responsibility, and consideration into your men and have them instill those same concepts into their men. If you get high enough in rank, and you have put your mark on your units as you have commanded them and instilled these concepts in all of your subordinates, you'll have an army of good men. When you finish your life here on earth and take stock of yourself and your accomplishments, you may be very surprised at how you've affected a great number of people, their careers, and their lives. The greatest accomplishment would be to know that you've made them better soldiers and better leaders.

There are more tired Corps and Division commanders than there are tired Corps and Divisions.

A lot of commanders think they have to make every decision, be in every conference, and be personally involved in every aspect and detail of an attack. This incorrect premise causes these commanders to expend a great deal of energy doing things they shouldn't be doing. It wears them out, causing them to be unnecessarily fatigued and eventually useless. Fatigue makes cowards of us all. Fatigue inflicts undue emotional stress, causing a commander to lose sight of his true mission. That's why you have a staff. Issue the necessary orders to them, delegate the authority and responsibility to them, and let them do their jobs and earn their paychecks. Of course, it's still your job to follow up and make sure things are done correctly, but it's the staff's job to carry out your orders. Don't do their jobs for them.

There is only one tactical principle which is not subject to change; it is, "To use the means at hand to inflict the maximum amount of wounds, death, and destruction on the enemy in the minimum amount of time."

You must hit fast, hit hard, and hit incessantly. Never stop your offensive. Attack, attack, attack. The time you save by killing the enemy quickly and unceasingly will be time that your soldiers won't have to spend in danger of losing their lives and suffering from the horrors of combat. Loss of lives in combat is unavoidable, but loss of time is criminal. There are commanders who will expend a specified ration of ammunition (and prolong an attack) over an extended period of time, knowing that such actions delay the winning of a battle. They will do this even though they know that by prolonging the battle they will expose their soldiers to risks for a greater period of time than is necessary. The reasoning behind this is to average out losses over a period of time so they won't look too high on reports. The good commander, on the other hand, will expend the same amount of ammunition in a very short period of time and get better results. Casualty figures will appear to be high for that short period, but overall, actual casualties will be less for the entire battle. The bottom line is that the report-conscious commander's daily losses will be less and will look good on reports (and in newspaper headlines) reflecting a single battle, and the good commander's daily losses will appear to be more. When viewed from the standpoint of an entire campaign or the whole war, however, the good commander's record will average out much better than the report-conscious commander's. An additional and highly positive benefit of this short-battle philosophy is that the good commander's soldiers won't be forced into a prolonged fight, and their time under fire will be shortened. This, in turn, decreases their chances of being wounded or killed. The good commander's soldiers will thus not be forced to suffer the fear, anguish, hunger, and psychological stress that the other commander's soldiers will, just to make the reports look good.

In a business sense, every resource must be used to maximum advantage to turn out a quality product. In some cases, resources are used not for product manufacture, but for the managers' six-figure salaries, perks, bonuses, and egos. Some examples are: a manager with the newest, fastest computer on his desk, which he rarely uses, while his secretary has an older model, which she uses constantly; accounting personnel who turn down requests for needed equipment because they don't like the verbiage on the request or because they don't want upper management to think they're spending too much money this quarter; and computer programmers who are pulled off a priority project to work on something for the CEO just so the MIS manager, the manager of information systems, can look good. One last example would be assigning those same programmers to a million-dollar project to fix a problem that could be done manually for next to nothing.

There is only one type of discipline, perfect discipline.

The dictionary says discipline is "training which corrects, molds, strengthens, or perfects." Any good commander will tell you that discipline is the lifeblood of an army. Without discipline, no organization or individual can function. In life, discipline is required to make a person a decent, honest, and valuable member of society. In business, discipline is required to make a satisfactory living from one's chosen profession. In an army, discipline is required to save lives, supplies, and time. In a combat situation, orders must be followed immediately and without question. Failure by subordinates to comply instantly with orders could very well mean not only the loss of lives but ultimately the loss of a battle. The loss of a battle, in turn, could ultimately cause the loss of a war, which could cause the loss of a nation's sovereignty. When plans are being made, there is ample time for people to make their opinions known and to offer their suggestions. When the planning is finished, however, and orders have been issued, there must be no disagreement or dissension. All must follow the same plan to the best of their abilities. Properly disciplined soldiers know this and accept it willingly.

There's a great deal of talk about loyalty from the bottom to the top. Loyalty from the top down is even more necessary and is much less prevalent. One of the most frequently noted characteristics of great men who have remained great is loyalty to their subordinates.

One of the most visible personal traits of the political officer is his utter lack of loyalty toward his soldiers. He'll kiss his superior's ass and crap on his subordinates if he thinks it will help his rise to power. Personal gain is his primary concern. He never asks, "Is this good for the army and for my men?" He invariably asks, "Is this a good career move? What's in this for me?" Far too many people at the top levels of command demand 100 percent from their subordinates yet never reciprocate as much as 1 percent. There's no way you can control what these egomaniacal morons do, but you can control what you do. When you attain high rank, don't forget what it was like at the bottom. Treat your men with the same loyalty and respect you would have expected and appreciated when you were a shavetail. It's your job to make sure loyalty and respect become part and parcel of the soul of your unit. It's imperative that you indoctrinate your men with the importance of loyalty. Continue with this process throughout your career and you will have infused this virtue in all your men, who, in turn, will deliver the message to their men.

War is not run on sentiment.

Waging war is the most serious and important job in the world. Ultimately, it's your nation at risk. There will undoubtedly be times when things must be done that will be abhorrent to any civilized individual, but they will be actions necessary for the survival of the country. There will be times when innocent lives will be lost, when great suffering will be visited upon the enemy and his countrymen, but it can't be avoided. A commander must make every attempt to keep from taking innocent lives, but not at the expense of losing a battle or the war. From the cradle to the grave, life, at best, is a constant struggle for survival. People will do what they must to protect themselves, their families, and their nation. Although you must be willing to die for your country, you must be more willing to kill for your country. War is a killing business. You must spill the enemy's blood, or he will spill yours.

A business cannot be run on personal feelings. It must make profits and avoid losses. Employees are not hired because they are friends; they are hired because they have ability.

War is simple, direct, and ruthless.

It takes a simple, direct, and ruthless man to wage war. If you aren't willing to kill people, don't choose a career in the military. If you aren't willing to order men into battle, knowing some of them will die, stay out. If you aren't willing to die at the hands of an enemy, stay out. If you aren't willing to destroy the enemy as ruthlessly as possible, stay out. The military establishment has no use for soft, nondedicated nonprofessionals.

Some Americans, for some unexplained and unintelligible reason, think that business is supposed to be fair. There is nothing fair about business. You must make the best product at the best price, and you must get it into the consumer's hands before the opposition does. You must constantly improve your product and keep ahead of the competition. If you don't, you won't stay in business. You must do everything humanly possible to remain in business short of performing illegal acts.

You must be single-minded. Drive for the one thing on which you have decided.

You can't let anything get in your way or stop you, whether it's the enemy or even your own high command. Once you've set your sights on a goal, every fiber of your being must be focused on it. You may have to cajole, flatter, and charm; you may have to display the world's worst temper and cuss a blue streak; you may have to do things that make you look like an A1 asshole— none of that matters. The main concern must be the mission. Driving and pushing will save lives. The harder you push, the more enemy will be killed. The more enemy you kill, the fewer of your soldiers will be killed. Pushing means fewer casualties and less suffering for your men. Don't stop until you've gained your objective.

You're never beaten until you admit it.

As long as you can fight, as long as you don't give up, you can never be whipped. Only death can stop you from doing your best. Even then, if you die well, your memory may make you a martyr, a standard bearer for your cause. The enemy may be able to crush your body, but it can never defeat an unconquerable soul. Never quit!

Suggested Reading

The following are only a few books that have been published on the subject of Gen. George S. Patton Jr. and his victorious U.S. Third Army. Some of them are out of print but might be found in used -bookstores or at collectible book shows. Out of the hundreds of books in the Patton Society's library, forty of them are specifically about Patton. Instead of listing and commenting on all of the Patton books in the library, I've listed only the ones that I found to be most valuable during my research into the Patton mystique.

Blumenson, Martin. *The Patton Papers.* 2 vols. Boston: Houghton-Mifflin, 1972–74. General Patton's personal papers are located at the Library of Congress. If you can't visit the library to study them, this book is a good alternative. Volume 1 contains the years 1885 through 1939. Volume 2 contains the years 1940 through 1945. Although I believe that Mr. Blumenson presumes a great deal at times and inserts his own psychological beliefs into the text, it's a good book for reading some of Patton's personal thoughts.

Deming, W. Edwards. *Out of the Crisis.* Cambridge, Mass.: MIT, 1982. If you want to know what quality control is and how it can be used to put the United States back on track, this is the first book you should read.

Essame, Hubert. *Patton: A Study in Command.* New York: Scribner's, 1974. It's interesting to note that the author comes to the conclusion that General Patton was one of the greatest battlefield commanders who ever lived—even if he wasn't British. In true British style, General Essame tells it the way he sees it. He's a great writer telling a great story.

Forty, George. *Patton's Third Army at War.* New York: Scribner's, 1978. This is an excellent history of General Patton and his Third Army. Reading this book will build a firm historical foundation for subsequent studies. It has lots of great photographs and gives a close-up view of the Patton style of war. Like General Essame, Lieutenant Colonel Forty is a great writer.

Koch, Oscar W. *G-2: Intelligence for Patton.* Philadelphia: Army Times Publishing Co., 1971. This is a great book. Not only does it give the reader some insight into Patton, but it also teaches a lot about the methods and value of intelligence work in the military.

Nye, Roger H. *The Patton Mind: The Professional Development of an Extraordinary Leader.* Garden City Park, New York: Avery, 1993. This is a great book that deserves to be in more than just military libraries. It belongs in the library of everyone who believes in proactive professionalism. Colonel Nye has done a superb job of assessing Patton's professional development relative to his voracious reading habit. Included are a large number of reproductions of actual pages from many of the military classics that Patton read, studied, and argued against. Many of the page reproductions show Patton's handwritten notes and commentaries. It's a truly fascinating book

Patton, George S., Jr. *War As I Knew It.* Boston: Houghton-Mifflin, 1947. This is Patton's story of his activity in World War II, sort of. It contains a wealth of knowledge and information about Patton, his thoughts, and his concepts of warfare. The only problem is that it really wasn't written by the general. Its contents are from Patton's letters and diaries. It was edited by Mrs. Patton, and all of the good parts were probably left out. The original texts were cleansed for publication, losing a great deal of the Patton fire and brimstone in the process. It should be in your library anyway.

Province, Charles M. *Patton's Third Army.* New York: Hippocrene, 1992. This is one of the most detailed historical accounts of the Third Army ever published. It's a daily chronology of the Third Army's advance through Europe from Normandy to Czechoslovakia—all 281 days of combat. Included is a chapter explaining the functions and responsibilities of an army's administrative services.

Province, Charles M. *The Unknown Patton.* New York: Hippocrene, 1983. Among other things, this book tells the true, inside stories about the slapping incidents, SHAEF's mistakes, Patton's philosophy, and his Secret of Victory.

Wallace, Brenton G. *Patton and His Third Army.* Harrisburg: Military Service, 1946. This is an honest, straightforward book lacking the usual sniping at personalities. It's one of the best books in the Patton Society's library. A lot of useful tactical information can be learned from this book.